Brown Girl, Brown Girl, Hasn't Anyone?

by
Michele Jeanmarie

Illustrated by Aaron Herrera

Archway Publishing books may be ordered through booksellers or by contacting:

Archway Publishing
1663 Liberty Drive
Bloomington, IN 47403
www.archwaypublishing.com
844-669-3957

Because of the dynamic nature of the Internet, any web addresses or links contained in this book may have changed since publication and may no longer be valid. The views expressed in this work are solely those of the author and do not necessarily reflect the views of the publisher, and the publisher hereby disclaims any responsibility for them.

Any people depicted in stock imagery provided by Getty Images are models, and such images are being used for illustrative purposes only. Certain stock imagery © Getty Images.

ISBN: 978-1-6657-4880-3 (sc)
ISBN: 978-1-6657-4881-0 (e)

Library of Congress Control Number: 2023915886

Print information available on the last page.

Archway Publishing rev. date: 08/17/2023

To mamá and daddy.

Diversity is distinction without a difference

Chela lived in a four-bedroom house in a small community called Rainbow City. Her house faced the clear blue waters of the Caribbean Sea. The second eldest of four girls, she enjoyed reading a lot.

At school, Chela was very involved. She participated in numerous school activities. She was even involved in the community. She wrote articles for the community's newspaper, *The Spillway*, with the help of her English teacher. She also enjoyed mathematics, especially geometry where lines, segments, triangles, and squares make up dodecahedrons, a favorite word of hers. Later to influence her gusto for contemporary art, Chela continued to challenge the chances of life.

She painted an abstract drawing which came in nowhere for she did not turn it in for doubting she would ever win! She memorized and rehearsed *The Ant's Picnic* but came in nowhere, for the day prior to the school wide competition, she became ill!

She outlined an oral composition, but cried and sobbed in front of the class for the topic was about something sad and painful.

She was asked to recite a soliloquy in Spanish in front of the school but feared she could not fare for fear she could not ferociously roll her r's.

Chela had given up! She would continue to do just a little bit more to make the honor roll, and that was just that.

6

At home, in front of her house, the community kids had gathered to play The Rat and the Cat.

Little rat, little rat! What are you doing in my cave?

Looking for something to eat.

With whose permission?

With mine!

Bet I eat you!

Bet you don't

Bet I do!

Bet you don't

Everyone got a chance to run around the circle. First it was Xiomara, then Roxana, then Carlota, then Carmen, then Yadira, then Yvette, then Suzette, then Amor, then Vielka, and then Maritza. Chela was not chosen, but she was happy because, at least, her little sister got chosen.

Chela had not said anything. She was glad it was dusk and time to go in. At 8:00, her favorite commercials would come on and summon her and her little sister to bed!

Let's go to bed
For we need our rest.
So that tomorrow
We can be our best.

The following day, after school, the kids of the community gathered at Chela's house. They chose to play *Matarile*. Two captains were chosen, and each picked their team members. Chela was last to be chosen, but she was happy because her little sister was chosen ahead of anyone.

Again, she had not said anything. She would quickly go in and see her favorite commercial once again. Tomorrow will be another and better day.

And it was!

It was during Physical Education and Chela's class had been assigned to volleyball. It was a tie game, and Chela's turn to serve. Everyone scurried and got extremely anxious and would not let Chela serve. Xiomara slid past Chela and posted up to serve. But, alas! The teacher turned around and caught her by surprise. She demanded that Chela served.

Chela nervously posted up. She gingerly held the ball in her left hand and swinging her right arm as far back as she could, forcefully struck the ball. Alas! It fell on the opponent's side. Chela's team had scored.

14

Chela was on top of the hill!

Successive days had gone by, and Chela's friends were not really Chela's friends.

Chela had found out that she would change school. She would start at an American school named after Christopher Columbus, *Cristóbal*, in Spanish.

Chela was excited. She would get to ride the school bus every morning to go to school. She would have new friends and new teachers. She knew the teachers would like her.

Pretty soon, the students at *Cristóbal* had gained her respect. She made honor roll. A roster was posted and Chela was ranked very high.

Soon, Chela began to play tennis. After school, she got her tennis paraphernalia and went to her old school in Rainbow City. There, a retired Physical Education teacher, Mr. Loney, coached her. She met him diligently and played tennis. She excelled and participated in several tourneys.

17

As time progressed, Chela had grown close to Julie, an American girl, who lived in the Canal Zone most of her life. In the morning, Julie would get off her school bus to meet her and together they would walk to classes.

News had broken that there would no longer be a Canal Zone. The Canal Zone would become extinct. Julie was very melancholic. As they were walking toward the girls' gymnasium, Julie had said to Chela that she was no longer her friend.

Chela marched on.

Christmas was soon approaching. Although Chela loved school, she too, was jubilant. She already knew one of the toys she and her little sister would get. She would get a brown doll, and her little sister would get a white doll.

After Christmas came *Carnaval*. Chela liked *Carnaval*. The town anxiously awaits this time of year. Chela's most joyous part of the *Carnaval* is the end of the parade. It is dedicated to the Soul Queen and her float, which was always spectacular. The Soul Queen is brown. She had to be brown. Every year, she was brown. This year she was also brown. She had to be the prettiest and the most popular of all the queens. As her chosen delegates paraded on, Chela admired her only with gaped mouth.

Chela's family decided to leave for the United States, after Lent. Chela was deliriously happy. She would have new friends and new teachers. She knew the teachers would like her.

In the States, she got good grades. The classes, she found, were easy. The teachers, she found, were amicable. The students, she found, treated her with indifference.

Whenever Chela spoke in English, she spoke with a heavy accent. She was asked to repeat the same thing several times. Chela was ashamed of the way she spoke. So she sought out new friends, friends who could speak Spanish. Chela was put in an advanced Spanish class. Soon, she was answering all the questions, making straight A's, helping the teacher translate documents. Chela's Spanish speaker friends were not really her friends.

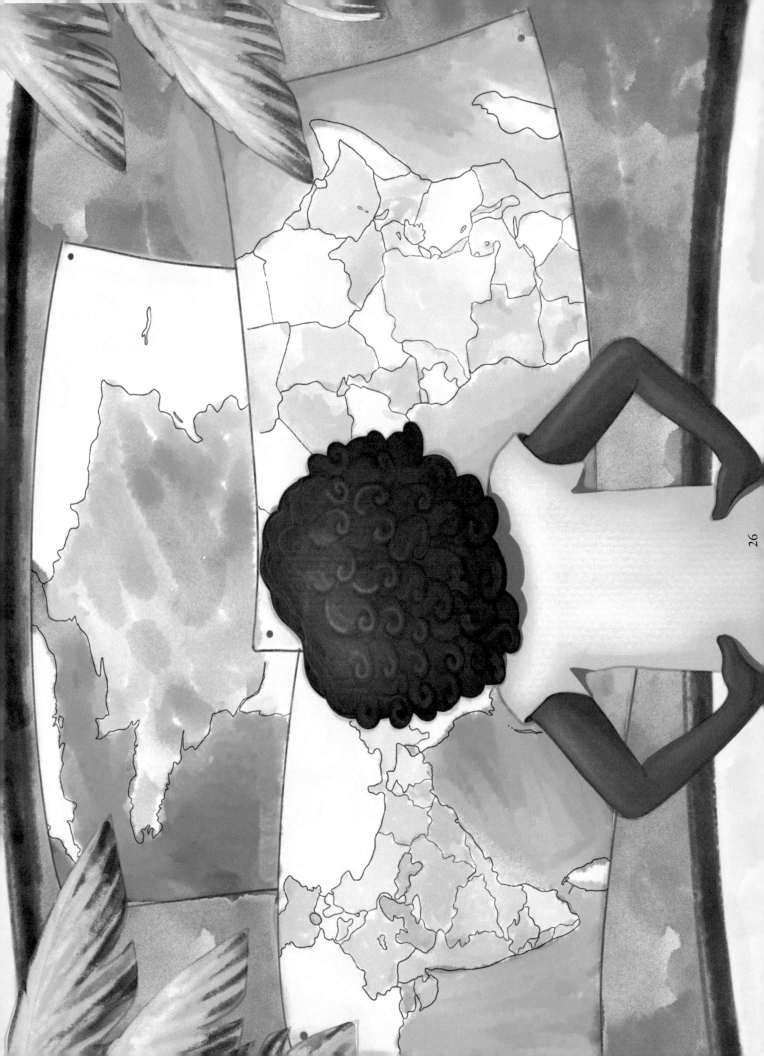

But who was this brown girl, anyway? Brown girl whose first language is English, born and raised in a Spanish speaking country, not knowing true friendship, child of an Afro-Hindu mother and Afro-French father.

Brown girl, brown girl, hasn't anyone?

Questions for Reflection

1. What perturbed Chela?
2. What games made a difference in Chela's life? Why?
3. List the turning points in Chela's life.
4. List Chela's strongest points.
5. List Chela's weakest points.
6. Research the significance of *Carnaval*.
7. Research the meaning of Lent.
8. Identify the historical period that may have contributed to Chela's feelings of dejection.
9. Make a dictionary of new words.
10. Define alliterations and list some examples from the text.

Current Events:

1. Research and define DACA.

2. Who would have been a DACA child in the story? Explain.

3. As an American, do you think she has any empathy for the DACA children that President Obama protected under his presidency? How has the wheel turned in history for the person in the story?

Printed in the United States
by Baker & Taylor Publisher Services